Barbie™

TAKES THE CATWALK

A STYLE ICON'S
HISTORY IN FASHION

KARAN FEDER

weldon**owen**

Contents

Introduction

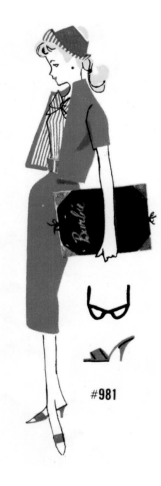

Fashion Catalog Booklet
Illustration, 1961

BUSY GAL

(without doll) #981
Two-piece red linen suit
with striped jacket lining.
Red-and-white striped
cotton sun-back blouse.
Open-crown hat, to match
blue belt and shoes.
Glasses. Two fashion drawings
inside artist's portfolio.
The set, $2.50.

#981

The Mattel Barbie doll came to be in 1959. Barbie was a teenager with a good job as a fashion model and an extensive wardrobe to rival that of all dolls that came before her. The state of the Barbie doll's modern clothes closet, one representing more than sixty years of sartorial spoils, is vast, intriguing, and the focus of my most recent preoccupation. As a fashion historian, I've been thinking about Barbie clothes and contemplating their significance. Do her fashion offerings actually reflect popular culture and mirror the evolving trends seen during the late twentieth century?

My investigation into this theme revealed a fascinating and profound narrative resulting in this groundbreaking publication. I credit the global coronavirus pandemic for the newfound downtime that afforded the opportunity to explore, pursue, and identify direct links, in precise historical context, between specific fashion-designer catwalk presentations, or significant cultural events, and an ensuing Barbie outfit.

My curiosity was amplified by the luxury of time and by the realization that my research was novel and could prove impactful to the Barbie-brand legacy. The Barbie sartorial canon boasts diverse references to French couturiers, American First Ladies, and popular musical stars, yet, curiously, does not include enthusiasm

#981
Busy Gal
1960
Worn by Ponytail Barbie

Representing ingenuity, self-expression, and fierceness, the fashion catwalk was, not surprisingly, an important inspiration for Barbie designers.

for the aesthetics of the original punk rock movement, or the deconstructed and avant-garde themes of the Japanese designers during the 1980s, nor the minimalist themes of the 1990s. I find the style trends that were not embraced by the brand to be just as fascinating as those trends that were accepted and marketed.

Broadly, this is a study of the Barbie doll's first forty years of fashion. That is, before the widespread availability of the Internet. The Internet changed everything. Omnipresent access to visual imagery spanning many centuries of sartorial history essentially leveled the fashion influencer playing field. Up to this point, the culture adhered to the authority of the established fashion industry and accepted their seasonal proclamations concerning narrative and silhouette. Post 2000, cultural exposure to the vastness of the Internet makes it impossible for the fashion industry to maintain control of the narrative. This invasion of disparate and viable style trends diluted any central theme in favor of the collective. The common fashionable trends of the 1950s, 60s, 70s, 80s, and 90s are decisive. It is more difficult to single out the trends that competently define the style statements of the ambiguous 2000s and 2010s. This publication is conceived to highlight Mattel's canny comment on culture and fashion via the sartorial offerings of Barbie from 1959 through 1999.

Of course, a thorough investigation of Barbie fashion is achieved only when the behind-the-scenes artisans of Mattel's design team are considered. These folks were paid to attend European couture runway shows, to study fashion magazines, and to analyze street-level trends with the goal of creating up-to-the-minute clothing for Barbie. Representing ingenuity, self-expression, and fierceness, the fashion catwalk was, not surprisingly, an important inspiration for Barbie designers. The collective genius of this design team is found in their ability to translate life-size styles and silhouettes into ensembles that are, at once, practical to manufacture and yet still recognizable once adapted to Barbie-scale. These skillful and innovative interpreters are expert at identifying and echoing the popular fashionable trends of any particular era.

#1794
Check the Suit
1970
Worn by Living Barbie

BASIC BARBIE DOLL
FASHION MODEL SET

Your Barbie doll is created of sturdy flesh-tone vinyl plastic. Moveable arms, legs and head make it easy to dress Barbie in her exciting fashion model's wardrobe. Barbie Doll, plus striped jersey swimsuit, sun glasses, pearl earrings and shoes... and special pedestal to keep Barbie on her feet for all Fashion Shows. **$3.00**

Notes on the Dolls Featured in This Book

- The descriptors "Ponytail," "Bubble-Cut" and "Swirl-Ponytail" (see pp. 14, 17, and 2) are consumer-created nicknames used to distinguish these Barbie dolls from one another. Mattel marketed all of these dolls with the same style number #850 and the same name, "Teen-age Fashion Model Barbie Doll."

- "American Girl" (see p. 35) is another consumer-created nickname. This doll was also marketed with the name "Teen-age Fashion Model Barbie Doll" but with the additional slogan "Lifelike Bendable Legs." This model also was given a new style number #1070.

- Julia (see p. 41) and Christie (see p. 89) were originally manufactured with black hair. The red-hued hair color seen on the dolls here is the result of a chemical reaction of the synthetic hair fibers caused by more than fifty years of exposure to natural and artificial light and the atmosphere. Typically, when an original Julia or Christie doll displays a hair color other than black, the transformed hair is referred to as "oxidized."

- The descriptor "Marlo-Flip" (see p. 42) is a consumer-created nickname that refers to the popular hair style worn by actress Marlo Thomas during the early years of her hit television series *That Girl* 1966-1971.

Fashion Catalog Booklet
Illustration, 1961

Barbie *Defined*

It was a strategic decision by the Barbie doll creator, Ruth Handler, to position the Barbie wardrobe at center-stage. The original Barbie doll retailed for three dollars and her first closet consisted of twenty-two marvelously detailed ensembles priced between one and five US dollars. Mattel calculated that, once the consumer acquired their Teen-age Fashion Model Barbie Doll, the bounty of trendy and tiny fashionable garments would entice continued ancillary purchases.

The original twenty-two Barbie looks featured themed ensembles with assigned names such as *Easter Parade, Suburban Shopper,* and *Winter Holiday.* These labels indicated each outfit's end use and sparked fantasy play patterns. The inaugural fashion collection, from *Undergarments to Wedding Set,* effectively served to define the Barbie personality.

The mechanics of clothing construction are a significant consideration for Barbie fashion designers. The original Barbie doll is roughly one-sixth human scale but the textiles used to make her clothing are manufactured in life-size scale. This insight offers explanation concerning the Barbie doll's disproportionately diminutive waistline. Typical clothing construction techniques such as darting, pleating, and gathering result in a finished garment that includes multiple layers of material. In order to represent a proportionately-looking figure once fully clothed, the doll required a waist measurement smaller than that calculated using a one-sixth ratio.

#850
Teen-age Fashion Model Barbie
1959
Worn by Teen-age Fashion Barbie

#986
Sheath Sensation
1961
Worn by Ponytail Barbie

Life-size dress
1958–1962
Compare with *Sheath Sensation*

14

The original Barbie doll is roughly one-sixth human scale.

Left
Ponytail Barbie
carry case
1961

Right
Barbie
carry case
1964

Couturier's Couturier

Cristóbal Balenciaga
Marie Claire magazine #66,
1960

Cristóbal Balenciaga is often described as a couturier's couturier. This moniker references Balenciaga's legacy and fame within the fashion design industry. The avant-garde silhouettes that distinguish his midcentury work were the product of his mastery of "the cut."

The designer's radical architectural shapes and dramatic sculptural simplicity during this period are credited for establishing the foundations of modernity that would ultimately develop into the minimalist aesthetic of the space age genre.

The fashion designers creating Barbie clothes were encouraged to follow prevailing sartorial trends and to seek inspiration within popular fashion boutiques. It is reasonable to expect that the design team was also influenced by visual references found within the lifestyle and fashion magazines of the period.

#954
Career Girl
1963
Worn by Bubble-Cut Barbie

Barbie doll's dramatic Red Flare evening coat and matching toque are likely inspired by Balenciaga's offerings from the early 1950s. The exaggerated silhouette of the sleeve is described as a melon or balloon sleeve. Cut a bit on the short side, this Balenciaga sleeve-style was ideal for showing off gloves and chunky wrist jewelry. Other design details of note are the stand-away collar and center-front bowknot. The look abandons any emphasis on the popular waist-defining silhouettes of the period and instead presents a trapezoidal form that widens from the shoulder to the hem. This silhouette foreshadows the "gamine look" and illustrates the couturier's architectural insight, and his fluid, graceful draping skills.

The look abandons any emphasis on the popular waist-defining silhouettes of the period.

Cristóbal Balenciaga
Sketch by Pierre Mourgue
L'Officiel #347, 1951
Compare with *Red Flare*

#939
Red Flare coat
1962

Sheath With Gold Buttons
dress
1962
Worn by Ponytail Barbie

Barbie doll's Career Girl tweed skirt-suit is another example likely inspired by the suits Balenciaga produced during the mid-1950s. The spread and rolled portrait-collar is draped and cut to stand away from the body, affording sufficient negative space to display neck ornaments. The outfit's matching hat mimics the designer's novel lampshade silhouette of the same era.

By offering Balenciaga-inspired outfits for the Barbie doll, the Mattel design team was communicating its expertise and understanding of forward-fashion. Barbie thus provides a positive affirmation for the concepts of individuality and self-expression.

Barbie thus provides a positive affirmation for the concepts of individuality and self-expression.

#954
Career Girl
1963
Worn by Bubble-Cut Barbie

Life-size skirt suit
Design by Cristóbal Balenciaga
1954
From the collection at the Victoria
and Albert Museum, London
Compare with *Career Girl*

The Barbie Black Magic Ensemble is modeled after a favorite dress from the personal closet of Ruth Handler, Barbie doll's creator. Handler's dress was likely inspired by the popular designs of Cristobal Balenciaga during the late 1950s and early sixties.

The skillful manipulation of transparent and opaque materials results in a harmonious presentation of inherently conflicting silhouettes. The complications found in producing an authentic lace textile at Barbie-scale no doubt necessitated the substitution of a plain net material to express lace-like qualities.

The Barbie Black Magic Ensemble is modeled after a favorite dress from the personal closet of Ruth Handler, Barbie doll's creator.

#1609
Black Magic Ensemble
1964
Design by Carol Spencer
Worn by Swirl-Ponytail Barbie

McCall's printed sewing pattern #4657
1958
Compare with Black Magic Ensemble

McCall's

PRINTED PATTERN

4657

SIZE 16
BUST 36

SHEER TRAPEZE AND SHEATH

75c
IN CANADA, 85c

First Lady *Fashion*

Oleg Cassini,
Jacqueline Kennedy's
"Secretary of Style"
January 1961

First Lady Jacqueline Kennedy's minimal, feminine, and modern fashion choices were dubbed "The Jackie Kennedy Look." This confident and sophisticated style was immediately embraced and emulated by American women. The look was defined by streamlined, monochromatic, A-line, and columnar silhouettes that were ornamented with uncomplicated details, such as statement-size buttons and bowknots. By the early 1960s, most American living rooms were furnished with a television set. Jackie Kennedy instinctively understood the value of dressing for the screen and selected an American fashion designer with a background in Hollywood costume design to serve as her couturier. Oleg Cassini helped Mrs. Kennedy define her public image and secure her legacy as one of the most influential and stylish women of the era.

Bell Dress
1962
Worn by Ponytail Barbie

Designed by Oleg Cassini for Mrs. Kennedy's use during an official visit to India, this is a splendid representation of the First Lady's modern style. The Barbie doll's Bell Dress mimics many of the design details seen in the Cassini look. Notice the frock's apricot color, the skirt's inverted front pleat, and the waist's statement bowknot.

Oleg Cassini helped Mrs. Kennedy define her public image and secure her fashion legacy.

Bell Dress
1962
Worn by
Ponytail Barbie

Oleg Cassini's apricot-colored dress was worn by Jacqueline Kennedy in March of 1961. The following year, a very similar replica of that dress went on sale in the Fall and Winter edition of the Sears, Roebuck and Co. catalog.

The Barbie version of the dress was also released in 1962. Sears elected to name its Cassini knockoff Bell Silhouette. The Mattel team similarly named its dress variant Bell Dress. Concerning the assigned names of these dresses, it is unclear if Sears provided inspiration for Barbie or if Barbie provided inspiration for Sears.

Sears, Roebuck and Co. Catalog,
pp. 36 and 37
Fall and Winter 1962
Compare with Bell Dress

7 Bell Silhouette moulde in fine acetate taffeta. Artfully seamed bodice . . skirt skillfully lined for shapeliness. In back: deep-V neckline, zipper. Dry clean. Wt. 1 lb. 2 oz. *Misses' sizes* 8, 10, 12, 14, 16. *State size.*
N31H 8046F—Light apricot
N31H 8047F—Light horizon blue......**$16.50**

Further evidence that the fashion-design teams at both Sears and Mattel were monitoring one another is realized in the similar color options for the Bell dresses. Both firms offered the dress in apricot and light-horizon blue colors.

Bell Dress in apricot and light-horizon blue
1962
Worn by Ponytail Barbies

In contrast to her predecessors, Jackie's style was typically devoid of decorative embellishment. Perhaps this was a deliberate gesture, one that was intended to communicate the seriousness with which she approached her position. Jackie aspired to be more than a decorative accessory on the arm of her husband, and she endeavored to serve as a contributing partner in the White House.

There is symbolism found in Mattel's selection of Jacqueline Kennedy as a role model. The First Lady was an impressive and intelligent woman with an acute understanding of fashion and its power to communicate.

There is symbolism found in Mattel's selection of Jacqueline Kennedy as a role model.

Campus Belle
1964–1965
Worn by Bubble-Cut Barbie

Life-size dress
Design by the House of
Bianchi, Boston, New York
1960
Compare with *Bell Dress*
and *Campus Belle*

John F. Kennedy was the youngest man to be elected president of the United States. In 1961, this portends the country's declining average age. By the mid-1960s, half the American population was under twenty-five years of age.

Jackie was just thirty-one when she became First Lady. Her nontraditional sartorial choices were modern and symbolic of a younger generation in the White House.

Her nontraditional sartorial choices were modern and symbolic of a younger generation in the White House.

Jacqueline Kennedy
Design by Oleg Cassini
July 1961
Compare with *Golden Glory*

#1645
Golden Glory
1965
Worn by Swirl-Ponytail Barbie

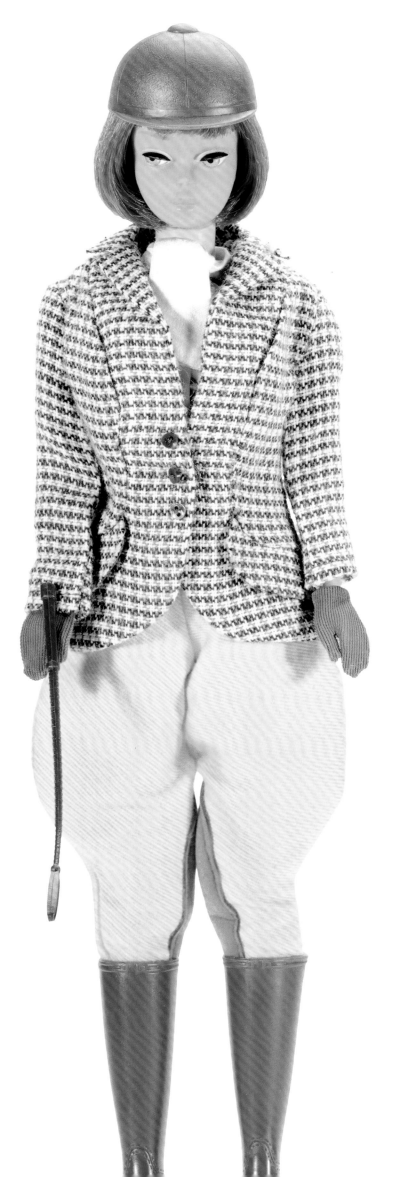

It is difficult to know, in fact, if Kennedy was the inspiration for the Barbie Riding in the Park equestrian ensemble, but there is sufficient anecdotal evidence to make a connection.

Carol Spencer, a fashion designer for Barbie, noted that she created the Barbie outfit titled Crisp 'n Cool in tribute to Jackie Kennedy's streamlined and fresh style. Indeed, the ensemble's name does lend itself to an accurate description of the First Lady's style sensibilities. This revelation offers a primary source account that serves to verify a direct exchange between Barbie fashion offerings and popular culture

Barbie received her first pet horse in 1971. Dancer was a beautiful chestnut-brown color and boasted bendable legs.

Jacqueline Kennedy
September 1962
Compare with *Riding in the Park*

#1668
Riding in the Park
1966
Worn by American Girl Barbie

It is quite possible that the Barbie fashion designers were inspired by the dramatic ensemble the new First Lady wore to the presidential inaugural ball in 1962. The name assigned to the outfit, *Formal Occasion*, does indeed hint at a reference to the historic celebration.

Alternatively, perhaps the Barbie team was inspired by the unique hooded cape from Jean Patou's Autumn/Winter 1964–1965 collection.

#1697
Formal Occasion
1967
Worn by Bubble-Cut Barbie

Design by Jean Patou
Autumn/Winter 1964–1965
Compare with *Formal Occasion*

Space Age

In 1961, US president John F. Kennedy, in an address to a special joint session of Congress, officially entered the country into the "Space Race." Kennedy's goal "— of landing a man on the moon and returning him safely to the earth" was to be achieved by the end of the decade. This national focus on space exploration, the future, and the unknown captured the imagination of fashion designers around the world.

Initiative, determination, and innovation are the principle themes of the space age. Barbie fashion designers adopted this sartorial space-age aesthetic and, in doing so, signaled the brand's empowering ideology.

#1641
Miss Astronaut
1965
Worn by Fashion Queen Barbie

Project Mercury American Astronauts
March 1960
Compare with *Miss Astronaut*

One of the more significant designers working during the decade of space exploration was the French couturier André Courrèges. His science-fiction fashion, which featured exacting geometric shapes employing metallic and shiny materials, appealed to the growing youth market. The designer's early training was realized at the House of Balenciaga, where Courrèges's penchant for streamlined construction techniques was sharpened.

Courrèges's science-fiction fashion, which featured exacting geometric shapes employing metallic and shiny materials, appealed to the growing youth market.

#1885
Salute to Silver
1969
Worn by Twist 'n Turn Julia

41

The Silver Polish ensemble was likely inspired by the collection André Courrèges presented in the fall of 1964. One distinct feature of this look is evident at the hemline of the pant legs. The unique notched detail from the Courrèges trouser is copied in Barbie doll's spacey jumpsuit. Of interest is the absence of a blouse with the Courrèges ensemble. It is not surprising that the Barbie team opted for modesty and revised the designer's uncovered presentation. The openwork midriff on Silver Polish is a clever solution that still alludes to bareness.

The unique notched detail from the Courrèges trouser is copied in Barbie doll's spacey jumpsuit.

#1492
Silver Polish
1969
Worn by Twist 'n Turn
Marlo-Flip Barbie

Design by André Courrèges
October 1964
Compare with Silver Polish

Life-size dress
1964–1968
Compare with
Salute to Silver

The original NASA spacesuits developed for the Mercury program were fabricated from a silver-tone material. As a result, the primary visual characteristic of 1960s-space-age fashion is defined by metallic-like textiles.

Closely resembling one of the youthful and angular silhouettes presented on the Courrèges catwalk in 1968, the Barbie Salute to Silver dress perfectly expresses the space-age aesthetic and the movement's cultural significance.

The Barbie Salute to Silver dress perfectly expresses the space-age aesthetic.

#1885
Salute to Silver
1969
Worn by Twist 'n Turn Barbie

Dressed in her drop-waist and streamlined shift featuring futuristic and high-tech-like materials, Barbie is suitably equipped for a quick trip to the moon.

Space exploration, the future, and the unknown captured the imagination of fashion designers around the world.

September 1966
Compare with *Intrigue*

#1470
Intrigue dress
1967
Worn by Twist 'n Turn Barbie

The space-age fashion silhouettes supported an active lifestyle and offered a modern version of femininity that focused on the sportswear inspired by the youth of the period. It's likely that the space-age movement nurtured the cultural atmosphere and set the stage in preparation for the reign of the influential youth culture. A central space-age theme is found in the enthusiasm for the unknown in service of a reworked definition of one's own reality. This concept ran parallel to the beliefs of the young people identifying as bohemians during the 1960s and 1970s.

The space-age fashion silhouettes supported an active lifestyle and offered a modern version of femininity.

#1470
Intrigue
1967
Worn by Twist 'n Turn Barbie

Life-size dress
Retailed by Marshall Field &
Company, After Five Shop
1964–1968
Compare with *Velvet Venture*

#1488
Velvet Venture dress
1969
*Worn by Twist 'n Turn
Marlo-Flip Barbie*

Synthetic textiles employing metallic-looking yarns were a design element of the space-age aesthetic. Such materials were viewed as futuristic and symbolized a forward-looking mindset wherein the fantasy of space exploration could become a reality.

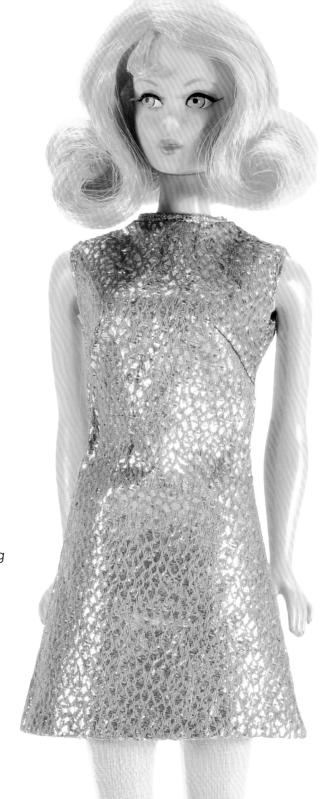

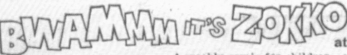

BWAMMM IT'S ZOKKO at

A weekly comic for children—ele[?]
style. That's how the producers de[?]
this completely new concept in children's
television. There'll be no regular intro-
ducers, at least no human one, for the
different items—or 'pages'—in the programme will be linked by the Zokko
pin-table who speaks with an electronic
voice. Making frequent comments at the
bottom of each page—rude or otherwise
—will be Mr. Zokko, a small cartoon
character. There'll also be a new space
fiction strip cartoon series about Skayn,
an astronaut hero who sets out to rescue
the Moon People from the menace of the
Far Side. The first programme includes
a fairground roundabout of brass band
instruments; the Tumblairs, a fast-mov-
ing trampoline act; a song; and a page of
jokes the more 'awful' the better.
So do make sure you place a regular
order with your television set NOW.

MR. ZOKKO

**Perhaps the Barbie space-age
Zokko! dress is related to
a space-fiction segment that
aired during the program.**

Zokko! print advertisement,
1968

This illustration appears in a
Mattel fashion catalog titled
"The World of Barbie Fashions
by Mattel" with a copyright
date 1966.

From 1968 to 1970, the British Broadcasting Corporation BBC aired a weekly children's television program called Zokko! It was billed as "television's first electronic comic" and is remembered as "defying description." The series was "hosted" by a talking pinball machine named Mr. Zokko. It is unclear if Mattel partnered with the production from the beginning, as the Zokko! outfit was already in the marketplace during the show's first season. Perhaps the space-age Zokko! dress is related to a space-fiction segment that aired during the program. The spaced-out storyline included a female character named Skayn. Could it be that Skayn was a futuristic space girl and she was illustrated wearing an outer-space costume similar to Barbie doll's Zokko? Unfortunately, most of the program's episodes have been lost to history.

#1820
Zokko!
1966
Worn by Hair Fair Barbie

During the late 1960s, Mary Quant, known for her youthful, spirited, and thoroughly modern clothing designs, launched a unique waterproof footwear collection. A brand advertisement from 1967 describes the "Quant Afoot" collection as boots "in crystal clear plastic over colours that zoom into fashion's orbit." Certainly, Quant's latest footwear designs were signaling themes of the space age. The moon girls who donned Quant's new boots would have the benefit of space travel in both comfort and style.

The Barbie design team introduced a bootie similar to Quant's Chelsea model in 1967. This space-age-chic bootie remained a part of the Barbie doll's closet into the 1970s.

#1484
Yellow Mellow stockings
1969

#3411
Poncho Put-On booties
1971
Worn by Hair Fair Barbie

Fashion designer Mary Quant
and models
1967
Compare with *Poncho
Put-On* booties

Youthquake

America's national character was jolted and transformed by the sizable, youthful generation of the 1960s. This seismic shift in the culture produced sartorial trends that served as symbolic visual statements proclaiming progressive and youthful innocence, while, at the same time, renouncing establishment authority.

Bouncy Flouncy's relaxed silhouette perfectly characterized the comfort and freedom integral to the youth movement. Youthful exuberance is further signaled in this dress with the repetition of "bouncy flouncies" and the playful, floral-print treatment.

Life-size dress
Design by Marjorie Scott Ott for Toby of Palm Beach
1965–1968
Compare with *Bouncy Flouncy*

#1805
Bouncy Flouncy
1967
Worn by Twist 'n Turn Barbie

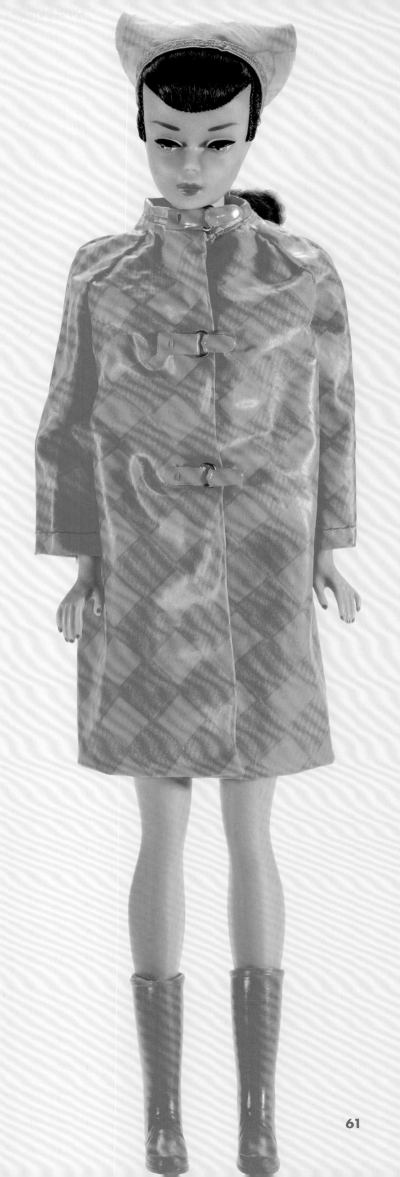

Drizzle Dash *is another outfit faithful to the "gamine look" of the 1960s and early 1970s. This rainwear ensemble, complete with its matching triangle scarf, is equally befitting a toddler or tweenager as it is a teenaged Barbie.*

French fashion models pose wearing rainwear and headscarves
September 1965
Compare with *Drizzle Dash*

#808
Drizzle Dash
1967
Worn by Swirl-Ponytail Barbie

All That Jazz *is a 1920s-revival silhouette originating from the societal era described as the "Jazz Age." Characterized by the lack of waistline and bustline definition, this style was a popular part of the gamine-look catalog. The drop-waist cut results in an adolescent and rectangular silhouette, rather than a mature, curvilinear silhouette.*

The drop-waist cut results in an adolescent and rectangular silhouette.

#1848
All That Jazz
1968
Worn by Talking Barbie

Design by Mary Quant
Spring 1964 collection
Compare with *All That Jazz*

Barbie fashion designer, Carol Spencer, attributes inspiration for the Lemon Kick ensemble to the revealing Scaasi pantsuit.

Life-size pantsuit
1968–1970
Compare with *Lemon Kick*

#1465
Lemon Kick
1970
Design by Carol Spencer
Worn by Talking Barbie

*The whimsical
Tunic 'n Tights outfit
does seem to embody
the personality of a
mischievous youngster.*

Here, the Barbie fashion designers borrow a theme from children's wear that dates back to the nineteenth century. This timeless, nautical look was worn by both boys and girls. See-Worthy, as the name suggests, is fundamentally a version of the traditional sailor suit. British fashion designer Mary Quant presented her interpretation of the sailor dress as early as 1961.

Perhaps the Mattel team was also influenced by a hit film released a year earlier. Funny Girl is a biographical musical about the burlesque comedian Fanny Brice. Brice, portrayed in the movie by actress Barbra Streisand, is seen costumed in a delightful sailor dress in one of the film's many memorable numbers.

British fashion designer Mary Quant presented her interpretation of the sailor dress as early as 1961.

Barbra Streisand in
Funny Girl
1968
Compare with *See-Worthy*

#1872
See-Worthy
1969
Worn by Twist 'n Turn Julia

The miniskirt silhouette was a radical departure from the acceptable skirt lengths of the previous decade. The silhouette has become an iconic symbol of the 1960s and represents the birth of a movement dedicated to the empowerment of women. The first miniskirt silhouettes for Barbie were introduced in the late 1960s.

The knee-high sock is a juvenile decoration employed on the expanse of bare leg that resulted from the miniskirt length. The knee-high is traditionally worn by children, but young women adopted the accessory as their own during the 1960s and 1970s. In further promotion of the era's gamine look, Barbie Style #3347 deftly imitates the trend.

The miniskirt silhouette was a radical departure from the acceptable skirt lengths of the previous decade.

#3347
From the *Best Buy Fashions* collection
1973
Worn by Walking Lively Barbie

The youthquake movement welcomed and embraced avant-garde forms of creative expression. The Color Kick skirt is an illustrative example of the movement's open-minded spirit. Here, Barbie sports an amusing miniskirt created from a vivid faux-furlike material.

The youthquake movement welcomed and embraced avant-garde forms of creative expression.

Fur fashion on the Baker's department store catwalk
January 1967
Compare with *The Color Kick* skirt

#3422
The Color Kick
1971
Worn by Hair Fair Barbie

Donning the mini silhouette served as a channel for young women to assert their individuality and was the spearhead for a fashion revolution. The radical skirt length raised eyebrows and pressured existing cultural norms defining appropriate exposure for women. This new silhouette offered women the freedom of self-expression, which, in turn, served to empower women to celebrate and expose their individual leggy female forms.

The name of this dress is likely a clever wordplay on an iconic slogan of the era, "Flower Power." Flower Power represented a nonviolent, counterculture movement in opposition to the Vietnam War. The babydoll-style Flower Wower dress might allude to the symbolism of the phrase, but it's unlikely that the brand was making any political statements.

This new silhouette offered women the freedom of self-expression.

#1453
Flower Wower
1970
Worn by Living Barbie

A contemporary woman (left) wears a youthful and bold patterned trapeze-shape minidress.
June 1968
Compare with *Flower Power*

The miniskirt and micro-miniskirt silhouettes gave rise to a few interesting and practical modesty garments. Hosiery, such as pantyhose, all-in-one nylon tights, and body stockings were options that designers presented to address the awkward moments of overexposure.
The leggy line that resulted from mini lengths provided a unique opportunity for designers to adorn the bare leg of the period.

The Color Kick ensemble features a witty, full-length body-stocking that simultaneously conceals and decorates.

The leggy line that resulted from mini lengths provided a unique opportunity for designers.

A model poses on the streets of Paris wearing an ensemble featuring cashmere tights by designer Alexandre Savin.
May 1964
Compare with *The Color Kick*

#3422
The Color Kick
1971
Worn by Hair Fair Barbie

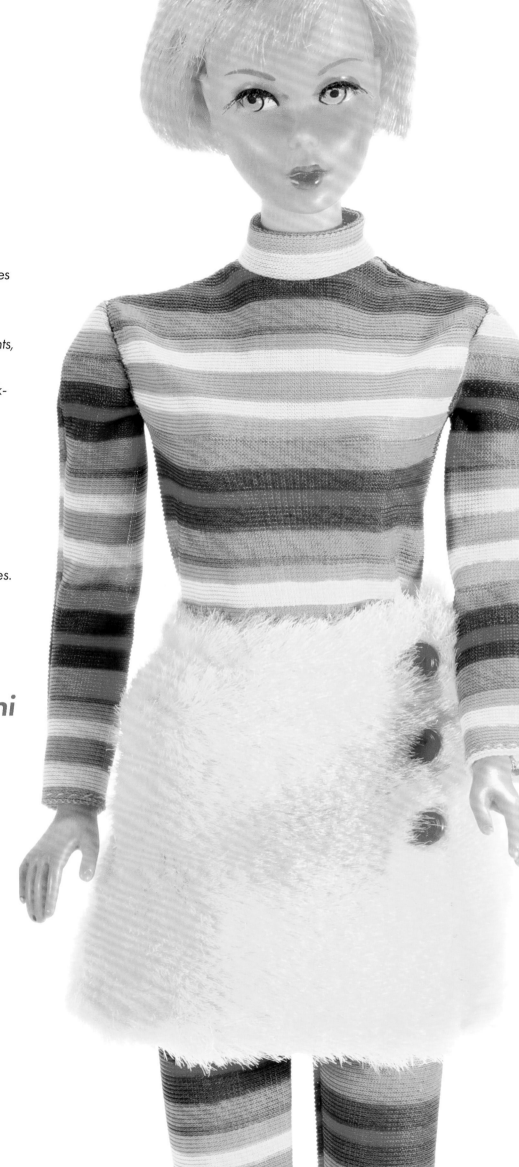

Psychedelic Mood

The psychedelic movement began in the mid-1960s and had a fascinating effect on many aspects of popular culture, including fashion. In Latin, psychedelic means "to awake the mind." In an attempt to express and portray the inner world of the psyche, the movement was informed by altered states of consciousness. The resulting visual art employed kaleidoscopic elements, abstract swirls, and paisley forms illustrated in vivid colors.

*The groovy Groovin' Gauchos ensemble (right) features
a fabric print inspired by the popular psychedelic art of the era.*

#1792
Mood Matchers
1970
Worn by Living Barbie

#1057
Groovin' Gauchos
1971
Worn by Talking Barbie

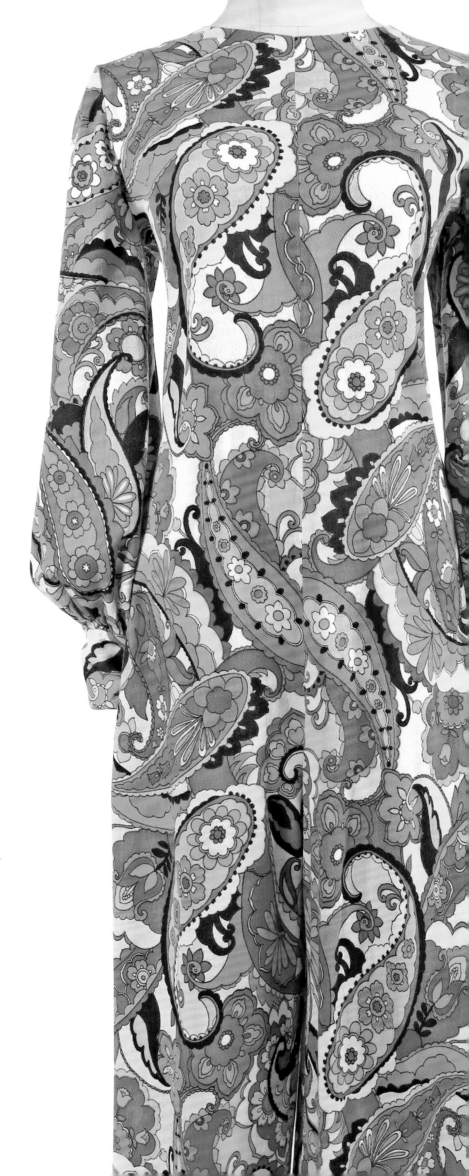

The catchy slogan "Turn on, tune in, drop out" was used by the psychedelic movement to describe its ideology. Simply put, the phrase instructed one to become sensitive, interact harmoniously, and detach from subconscious attitudes.

Psychedelic visual art employs kaleidoscopic elements, abstract swirls, and paisley forms.

Life-size jumpsuit
1967–1970
Compare with *Pajama Pow*

#1806
Pajama Pow
1967
Worn by Twist 'n Turn Barbie

85

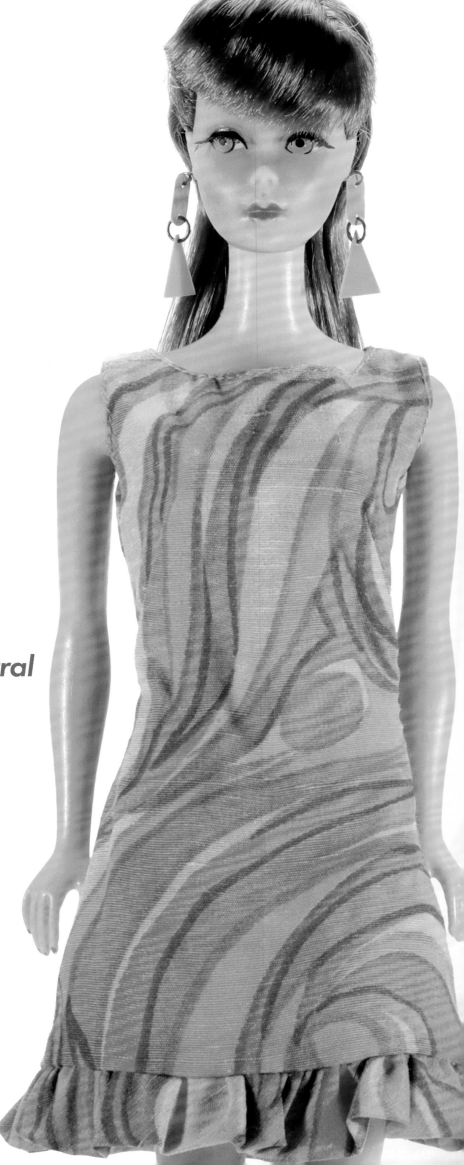

Here, the name of the Swirly Cue dress expertly describes a central visual element of the psychedelic-art genre (swirls) and is likewise a delightful adaptation of the word "curlicue."

Note the Barbie-doll scale of this printed material. If the appropriate fabric could not be sourced in the marketplace, the Mattel design team developed a custom textile print to suit the doll's unique proportions.

The Swirly Cue dress expertly describes a central visual element of the psychedelic-art genre.

#1822
Swirly Cue
1968
Worn by Twist 'n Turn Barbie

Life-size dress
1966–1969
Compare with *Swirly Cue*

AUGUST 21 · 1970 · 50¢

Life magazine
August 21, 1970

On the cusp of a new decade, fashionable women were distressed by a hemline crisis.
Designers had provided no clear direction or pronouncement in the matter of the most modern and stylish skirt length. During the early 1970s, women were afforded the vexing options of a micro-mini-, a mini-, a midi-, or a maxi-length skirt.

Pictured on the cover of *Life* magazine dated August 21, 1970, is a photograph of a young woman wearing a miniskirt. She is viewed from behind while gazing into a full-length mirror, and she positions a midi-length skirt at her waist for consideration. The accompanying article warns "It will soon be farewell to knees and maybe even calves."

#3357
Silver Blues top coat
#3357
Fancy That Purple hot pants
#3362
1972
Worn by Twist 'n Turn Christie

89

This graduated lineup presents the diverse skirt-length
options for the Winter 1970 fashion season.
Paris, August 1969

Compare with varied hem-lengths seen during the late 1960s
and early 1970s on the following page

During the early 1970s, women were afforded the vexing options of a micro-mini-, a mini-, a midi-, or a maxi-length skirt.

#3485
Madras Mod
1972
*Worn by Walk Lively
Miss America Barbie*

#1799
Maxi 'n Mini
1970
Design by Carol Spencer
Worn by Living Barbie

#1869
Midi-Magic
1969
*Worn by
Twist 'n Turn Barbie*

In support of the bohemian ethos, American youth culture embraced national folk dress from external cultures. Assorted design elements unique to regions in Africa, Asia, Central America, Europe, and North America were borrowed and haphazardly incorporated into the youth wardrobe. From the bohemian point of view, these stylistic seizures flaunt a sympathetic willingness to explore and try on unfamiliar cultures. The fringing detail featured on the Turtle 'n Tights skirt is inspired by a technique seen in traditional Native American garb. The artisanal themes of the indigenous peoples of America were adopted by the counterculture movement in compassionate support of the community's modern-day plight.

In support of the bohemian ethos, American youth culture embraced national folk dress from external cultures.

The skirt at left features a popular fringing detail reminiscent of Native American artisanal techniques.
June 1970
Compare with *Turtle 'n Tights*

#3426
Turtle 'n Tights
1971
Worn by The Sun Set
Malibu Barbie

The bohemians' use of national folk dress highlighted traditional decorative embellishments and techniques unique to specific regions. Embroidered and woven details executed by Native artisans are prominent in this genre and signal a consciousness of the efforts of artisans and their craftsmanship. Clothing that is homemade and handmade supports the movement's general rebellion against the established rules of propriety. The fabrication of the In Stitches pant suit is inspired by the work of traditional Guatemalan weavers.

The fabrication of the In Stitches *pantsuit* is inspired by the work of traditional Guatemalan weavers.

Gloria Steinem
December 1971
Compare with *Good Sports*

By origin, working-class denim garments were conceived to serve men's functional needs. The bohemian movement rejects tradition when denim garments are donned by both men and women in equal measure. Denim clothing serves to symbolize the questioning of society's gender stereotypes and is a visual affirmation of women's liberation from expected convention.

The Good Sports denim jeans feature the new and trendy "hip-hugger" pant style wherein the waistline is dropped to hip level.

The bohemian movement rejects tradition when denim garments are donned by both men and women in equal measure.

#3351
Good Sports
1972
Worn by Living Barbie

In an expression of the bohemians' nostalgia for a bygone existence, the clothing that was worn "on the prairie" by the late nineteenth-century pioneers of the American West served as a pervasive inspirational style statement. This theme implied that a past time period is more perfect and, thus, more authentic than the present age. The "prairie" look was typically illustrated in a silhouette characterized by a gathered midi- or maxi-length skirt, a puffed sleeve, an unassuming square or high neckline, a feminine ruffle, and lace details.

The name assigned to the Victorian Velvet outfit communicates that Mattel is conscious of the origins of the "prairie" revival look.

The name assigned to the Victorian Velvet outfit communicates that Mattel is conscious of the origins of the prairie revival look.

#3431
Victorian Velvet
1971
Worn by Walk Lively Barbie

Life-size dress
1968
Design by Carol Lisy
Compare with *Victorian Velvet*

To the bohemians, an uncomplicated and modest rural existence was a defiant lifestyle choice; it embraced the idea of "returning to nature" and supported the basic tenets of the environmental, or "back-to-the-land," movement. The experimental communes of the era were in pursuit of this ideal and were symbolic of an anti-capitalist principle.

The Laura Ashley and Gunne Sax brands realized tremendous commercial success with their stylized interpretations of this romanticized look back at history.

An uncomplicated and modest rural existence was a defiant lifestyle choice.

#3205
From the *Best Buy Fashions* collection
1973
Worn by Quick Curl Barbie

January 1970
Compare with *Best Buy Fashions* #3205

The A-line evening gown features a unique and distinctive organza boa quite similar to one Givenchy exhibited in a 1973 collection.

Significant to the growth of the disco craze, and perhaps resulting from it, were the opening of the discotheque Studio 54 and the release of the film Saturday Night Fever. Both events occurred in 1977, and both spread the iconic stylistic themes of the era all around the globe. Television and print media never missed an opportunity to report on the celebrities seen at "Studio."

Hubert de Givenchy, the French couturier best known for his lifelong collaboration with film actress Audrey Hepburn, was the likely inspiration for this Barbie ensemble. The A-line evening gown features a unique and distinctive organza boa quite similar to one Givenchy exhibited in a 1973 collection.

#9837
Dramatic Black and Silver Shimmer!
1977
Worn by Superstar Barbie

Life-size dress
1974–1977
Compare with *Dramatic Black and Silver Shimmer!*

A figure-hugging look by
the French haute couture
House of Torrente
Spring/Summer 1973
Compare with *Best Buy
Fashions* #9967

The design work of Biba, Givenchy, Halston, and Yves Saint Laurent define this moment in time. Each of these brands is inspired, in part, by the elongated close-fitting 1930s silhouette. The 1970s version of a 1930s Hollywood-glamour look is achieved with slippery synthetic materials, liquid-jersey knits, slinky fibers, and highly reflective yarns, all of which added drama while also complementing the body in motion. These fabrics offered a sparkly and fluid presentation, while serving the functional requirements of "doin' the Hustle."

#9967
From the *Best Buy Fashions* collection
1977
Worn by Superstar Barbie

The contrasting metallic gold-tone element seen at the neckline of the Barbie two-piece dress was likely intended to imitate a cowl-style necklace fabricated from a linking, metal-mesh material. Fashion brand Whiting and Davis expertly incorporated this specialized metal material into the designs of sensual garments and accessories. The reflective character and fluid movement of the mesh completely captured the essence of the disco era.

The reflective character and fluid movement of the metal mesh completely captured the essence of the disco era.

#2550
From the *Best Buy Fashions* collection
1978
Worn by Superstar Barbie

Life-size dress, necklace, and belt
Necklace design by Anthony Ferrara
for Whiting and Davis Company
1975–1980
Compare with *Best Buy Fashions* #2550

Just like the iconic mirrored disco ball, Lurex textiles captured and reflected light in a dramatc fashion.

The simple and columnar line of the Barbie disco dress represents fashion-designer Halston's body-conscious approach to design. The fabrication features knit yarns with a metallic appearance and references a consequential material of the era known as Lurex. Just like the iconic mirrored disco ball, Lurex textiles captured and reflected light in a dramatic fashion.

During the 1970s, Halston offered a skull-cap silhouette in a number of color and material variations, including styles covered with sequins. This Barbie cap imitates this trend, which represents the influence of the 1930's revival in fashion.

#9720
Original outfit for Superstar Barbie
1978
Design by Carol Spencer
Worn by The Sun Set Malibu Barbie

Life-size dress and cap
Design by Norman Berg for Denise Fashions
1971–1976
Compare with the original outfit for Superstar Barbie

The 1970s belong to Halston.

This Barbie ensemble embodies design elements seen in the work of both Halston and Yves Saint Laurent during the 1970s. The Halston style was chic, effortless, minimalistic, yet luxurious, and the designer is remembered as American fashion's first superstar. The designer was frequently seen at Studio 54, where his celebrity, as well as his work, contributed to the excitement of the sensational Manhattan nightclub. The fashion-industry trade journal Women's Wear Daily, notably declared that "the 1970s belong to Halston."

The chubby-style jacket was a garment popularized by Yves Saint Laurent and Halston during the 1970s. These dramatic jackets were made from fur or feathers and provided a striking contrast in silhouette when paired with the slinky gowns of the era.

#2481
Dramatic Blue and Silver Aglitter!
1978
Worn by Superstar Barbie

Supermodel Cheryl Tiegs
Chubby jacket design by Halston
December 1978
Compare with *Dramatic Blue and Silver Aglitter!*

It is likely that the Barbie design team was well aware of Biba. Described less as a fashion label and more as a way of life, the Biba brand was sold at its London-based boutique and through the shop's mail-order catalog. Designer Barbara Hulanicki deftly provided young, creative looks that were trendy, yet affordable. The Barbie trumpet-style skirt showcases the graphic, fluid, and bias striping of the 1930s-revival silhouette. The signature swirl of the contrasting panels was particularly effective in emphasizing dance-floor movement. This design detail was a huge commercial success, and the market offered many interpretations in dresses and skirts throughout the 1970s.

Designer Barbara Hulanicki for Biba deftly provided young, creative looks that were trendy, yet affordable.

Life-size two-piece ensemble
1971
Compare with *Best Buy Fashions* #7209

#7209
From the *Best Buy Fashions* collection
1975
Worn by The Sun Set Malibu Barbie

More Is More &
Less Is Less

Designer Nolan Miller
November 1985

Designer Nolan Miller was just finishing up his gig with the hit television series *Charlie's Angels* when producer Aaron Spelling invited him to design the costumes for *Dynasty*. The production's extraordinary wardrobe budget occasionally ballooned to $35,000 per episode. That figure is equivalent to more than $100,000 in today's dollar value. The costume designer reportedly never repeated a look during the nine-season series. Miller was rewarded with Emmy nominations four years in a row 1983–1986.

It is likely that the Mattel design team embraced the culture's fascination with *Dynasty* and tuned in, along with the rest of the nation, to see what everyone was wearing. Today, *Dynasty* is considered a defining television program of the decade.

#7956
From the *Twice as Nice Reversible Fashions* collection
1985
Worn by Happy Birthday Barbie

The success of the primetime-television soap-opera format of the late 1970s (Dallas premiering in 1978 and Knots Landing in 1979) paved the way for the release of Dynasty in 1981. Each of these popular television series exposed and celebrated the lifestyles of the upper class and, in so doing, provided an aspirational roadmap for Americans to navigate a new decade that would be defined by "more."

The Dynasty narrative was symbolic of America's obsession with more. That is, more wealth, more success, more luxury, more glamour, and, ultimately, more power. For better or for worse, the self-reflection of the 1970s was devoured by the self-indulgence of the 1980s.

The gigot-style sleeve of this Barbie dress accentuates the drama of the shoulder line in a design that perfectly illustrates the era's popular triangular silhouette.

The gigot-style sleeve of this Barbie dress accentuates the drama of the shoulder line in a design that perfectly illustrates the era's popular triangular silhouette.

#9146
From the *Spectacular Fashions* collection
1985
Worn by Loving You Barbie

Joan Collins in *Dynasty*
March 1983
Compare with *Spectacular Fashions* #9146

**The exaggeration of
the sleeve structure served
to artificially enhance
the shoulder line.**

Miller's work for Dynasty connected with the zeitgeist of the era, and popular demand resulted in retail offerings for the commercial masses. Both "The Dynasty Collection" and "The Dynasty Fur Collection" were womenswear lines based on the costumes Miller created for the show's lead actresses.

The flamboyant and exuberant sleeve treatment of this Barbie outfit was also seen on the Dynasty set. The exaggeration of the sleeve structure served to artificially enhance the shoulder line and to emphasize the triangular silhouette of the period. Inherent in this silhouette is the calculation that a distorted and wide shoulder line will result in the optical illusion that appears to diminish and narrow both the waist- and hiplines.

Dynasty cast members
Designs by Nolan Miller
1981
Compare with *Twice As Nice Reversible Fashions* #7956

#7956
From the *Twice as Nice Reversible Fashions* collection
1985
Worn by Happy Birthday Barbie

The sartorial offerings for Barbie during the 1980s illuminate an underlying narrative that concentrates on establishing her character as a successful role model who has decisively attained the era's fantasy of "having it all."

This impressive ensemble boasts not one, not two, not three, but TEN unique looks that might be created with the numerous fox-fur-like components. Here, Barbie surrenders to a central theme of the era—that when it comes to luxury goods, more is definitely more.

#7093
Original outfit for Fabulous Fur Barbie
1983
Worn by Magic Curl Barbie

A model presents a midi-length fur coat designed by Bill Gibb. In attendance is the late Princess Margaret (left).
March 1977
Compare with the original outfit for Fabulous Fur Barbie

The bountiful use of vigorous ruffle treatments is a dominant design detail used during the period. This treatment creates a silhouette that is grand and dramatic in scale and serves as a visual symbol of the decade's "more-is-more" theme. Barbie fashion designers earnestly embrace this idea in all manner of flouncy applications.

Life-size dress
Design by Tadashi
1986–1988
Compare with the original outfit for
Perfume Pretty Barbie

#4551
Original outfit for Perfume Pretty Barbie
1988
Worn by Perfume Pretty Barbie

His design strategy confronted the brand's iconic "Chanel-isms."

In the early 1980s, French legacy brand Chanel was modernized with the appointment of a new chief designer, Karl Lagerfeld. His design strategy confronted the brand's iconic "Chanel-isms" in an effort to reinterpret its visual legacy statements for a younger and hipper customer. Lagerfeld effectively and brilliantly resuscitated an uninspired couture house by embracing the past and bringing it into the future. Aggressively exploiting legacy logos and design elements, the deconstructed and reconsidered Chanel brand was soon perfectly suited to the exhibitionism inherent in the era of status dressing.

Yves Saint Laurent
1992

#6558
From the *Paris Pretty Fashions* collection
1990
Worn by Wedding Fantasy Barbie

Here, the Barbie design team is inspired by French couturier Yves Saint Laurent. The Spring/Summer 1988 collection from Saint Laurent is remembered as a celebration of the splendor and luxury of couture. The designer presented a series of joyous pieces displaying intense and intricate embroidery treatments. A few standouts were inspired by the paintings of Vincent van Gogh, namely Sunflowers and Irises. The bright colors, bold prints, and dense embellishment seen in these looks serve as an expression of the decade's excesses.

The Barbie design team deftly echoes Saint Laurent's silhouette, fabrication, and his catwalk styling in this elegant evening skirt suit. Lest one wasn't convinced of the Barbie team's good taste, Mattel declares this fashion collection Paris Pretty Fashions.

The Barbie design team deftly echoes Saint Laurent's silhouette, fabrication, and catwalk styling.

#6558
From the *Paris Pretty Fashions* collection
1990
Worn by Wedding Fantasy Barbie

Designs by Yves Saint Laurent
Spring/Summer 1988
Catwalk presentation: January 1988
Compare with *Paris Pretty Fashions* #6558

150

This dramatic evening gown is another example of Mattel's designers looking to the endorsed European tastemakers for inspiration. The unique silhouette of this gown was seen on a number of fashion runways during the 1980s, including those of Yves Saint Laurent and Emanuel Ungaro. The Barbie doll's exuberant hat might have been inspired by Ungaro's Autumn/Winter 1983 catwalk presentation. The ensemble perfectly exemplifies the operatic theatricality of popular fashion during the opulent decade.

This dramatic evening gown is another example of Mattel's designers looking to the endorsed European taste-makers for inspiration.

#4512
From the *Private Collection Fashions* collection
1988
Worn by Crystal Barbie

Design by Yves Saint Laurent
Autumn/Winter 1982–1983
Catwalk presentation: July 1982
Compare with *Private Collection Fashions* #4512

Women entering the traditional male-dominated work environment were confronted with the predicament of what to wear. The nearly elusive pursuit to express a feminine image of assertiveness, authority, confidence, and determination, while simultaneously affecting a distinctive and fashionable look that was devoid of aggression and intimidation, produced a corporate uniform termed "the power suit." A successful power suit is: impeccable, yet unthreatening; flattering, yet conservative; fashionable, yet practical; and masculine, yet feminine.

Design by Yves Saint Laurent
Spring/Summer 1984
Catwalk presentation: October 1983
Compare with *Dress Designer*

#9081
Dress Designer
1985
Worn by Peaches 'n Cream Barbie

Music-Video
Star Style

The Music Television Network, known as MTV, debuted in 1981 as a cable television network devoted to presenting pop music videos, related bits of musical industry news, and reports on the fashions and lifestyles of popular musicians. Much more than simply a radio station with pictures, MTV offered a radical and modern way for young adults to experience pop music. The innovative format provided a convenient round-the-clock, seamless, and intimate form of communication between musician and fan. Musicians eager to establish a memorable visual identity quickly discovered the value of, and the revolutionary power of, the three-minute music video.

MTV served as the ideal tool for publicizing star style and penetrating popular consciousness. As a result, the music channel was instrumental in the communication of pop-culture fashion trends to the youth of the 1980s.

In contrast to the decade's adherence to the themes of the status-dressing movement or the power-dressing movement, pop musicians elected to adhere only to their own individualistic style statements. They promoted a freedom of the individual spirit and developed an amalgam of looks that were inspired by street-level youth who were employing a mash-up of garments from past, present, and future. The mainstream acceptance and adoption of these style statements created a new and commercially legitimate market segment within the fashion industry. The broad range of looks promoted by pop musicians mandated a broad assortment of style options. Most significantly, this was neither a trend assortment nor a market category that was dictated by the couturiers.

Recognizing the cultural influence of MTV, the Barbie team released a series of music-inspired fashion collections.

#3394
From the *Concert Tour Fashions* collection
1987
Worn by Sun Gold Malibu Barbie

157

Madonna's commercial success within the entertainment industry, coupled with her "heavy rotation" on MTV, generated a powerful and global platform from which the performer was able to influence mainstream popular consciousness. Madonna invented a unique stage wardrobe that provided a visual template for many of the iconic style statements of the 1980s. One of those trends is expressed in the Barbie outfit on p. 157— the flirtatious concept of underwear-as-outerwear is deftly delivered in the lacey bustier-corset.

In celebration and promotion of the excellence portrayed in music video productions, MTV introduced a new category in yearly award-show concepts. The inaugural edition of MTV's Video Music Awards (VMAs) was presented in 1984, three years following the cable network's debut. As a featured artist on the awards show, American singer and songwriter Madonna performed her new album's title song, "Like a Virgin," dressed in a rebellious and revealing interpretation of a wedding gown. A highlight of the unconventional and unforgettable performance featured the "bride" crawling and rolling sinuously around the stage floor. This single performance would prove to be a defining moment, not just in pop-culture history, but also for Madonna and the VMAs.

#2688
From the *Barbie and the Rockers*
Fashions collection
1986
Worn by Dream Glow Barbie

Madonna at the MTV Video Music Awards
September 1984
Compare with *Barbie and the Rockers*
Fashions #2688

Fantasy *Futurism*

Thierry Mugler
1984

A recurring theme in the work of Thierry Mugler is discovered in his questioning of the traditional and his desire to define the look of the future. The designer's clothes offered women a whole new language with which to express femininity. Highly engineered patterning created angular, yet curving silhouettes that would prove decidedly influential throughout the decade and into the next. Mugler's "space age vixens" were likely inspirational in the context of the Barbie fantasy futurism look.

Mattel's designer Carol Spencer cites the French ready-to-wear label designed by Thierry Mugler as the source for the Barbie collection of fantasy space outfits marketed as *Barbie Astro Fashions*. Broadly, the Mugler inspiration affirms that the Barbie design team kept current with the work of various European fashion designers. Although it was understood (dictated by market research) that this design challenge would be fantasy-driven, Spencer goes the extra mile by researching contemporary fashion collections and selecting trendy design elements to employ in a unique expression of the genre and the era.

Happily, Mattel's earlier strategy of assigning clever names to the outfits is revisited with this Astro Fashions collection. A series of outer-space themed titles such as Welcome to Venus, Space Racer, and Galaxy a Go Go, express the playful nature of Barbie doll's adventures in space.

#2743
Dazzling Dancer
1985
Design by Carol Spencer
Worn by Sunsational Malibu Barbie

Parisian Pouf

The work of French couturier Christian Lacroix masterfully expressed the spirited excess that was valued during the 1980s and early 1990s. Determined to enchant, Lacroix's genius is defined by a sophisticated riot of colors, lavish artistic embellishments, and an operatic blending of disparate surface patterns, luxurious trims, and overall ecstasy-of-ornament. One of the most significant fashion designers of the era, his intriguing and visionary clothing served as a main epicenter of the era's sartorial scene.

One memorable and influential idea that is credited to Lacroix is the "pouf" silhouette. Broadly defined as simply a bouffant style, the pouf silhouette is characterized by a puffed-out, inflated area that was typically executed in the skirt section of the dress. The pouf might be placed at center-back in a bustle-like statement or seen at each side-seam in a Marie-Antoinette-like statement. Curiously, the pouf also made a forward-facing appearance in an especially witty statement. Overflowing with coquettish charm, Lacroix's pouf dresses (also called puffball dresses) were a sensation during the second half of the decade.

Christian Lacroix
October 1987

This delightful outfit from the Paris Pretty Fashions collection is quite similar to a dress shown in 1987 that was created by Maison Lacroix. This Barbie ensemble thoroughly captures the coquettish charm inherent in the couturier's work from the era. Akin to Lacroix's creation, this Barbie dress generally adopts the pouf concept and, additionally, mimics a floral rose pattern, a strapless bodice with bowknot detailing, tulle underskirt, and the unusual separate and detached sleeves. Further emulating the Lacroix-look, this pouf dress is topped with a dramatic, cartwheel-style hat.

This Barbie ensemble thoroughly captures the coquettish charm inherent in Lacroix's work from the era.

#1909
From the *Paris Pretty Fashions* collection
1989
Worn by Fabulous Fur Barbie

Design by Christian Lacroix
October 1987
Compare with *Paris Pretty Fashions* #1909

169

Christian Lacroix's original and refreshed expression of haute couture produced garments of grandeur fused with a knowing whimsy. This modern interpretation appealed to the newly wealthy generation of shoppers who wanted to dress up to show off their status.

One immediate similarity observed when comparing the Barbie ensemble with the Lacroix-designed cocktail dress is the playful and eye-catching heart-shaped detail positioned at the center-front of the bodice. Additionally, both offer a floral surface pattern, a strapless bodice, and a flared peplum.

Design by Christian Lacroix
October 1987
Compare with *Paris Pretty Fashions*
#1911

#1911
From the *Paris Pretty Fashions*
collection
1989
Worn by Crystal Barbie

Bouffant and gravity-defying concoctions proved particularly popular with the teenaged junior market.

#8242
From the *Fantasy Fashions* collection
1990
Worn by UNICEF Barbie

Life-size dress
Design by By Choice
1986–1989
Compare with *Fantasy Fashions* #8242

172

At the end of the 1980s and transitioning into the early 1990s, the flirtatious charm that the Parisian couturiers delivered in their bouffant and gravity-defying concoctions proved particularly popular with the teenaged junior market. A number of manufacturers translated Lacroix's lavish hallmark style into affordable occasion dresses designed to meet the trendy needs of high school prom celebrations. A bounty of flirty ruffles and youthful bowknots often decorated these memorable, and teenager-approved, special occasion dresses.

By Choice
DRESS

SIZE 7
MADE IN U.S.A.   OVER FOR CARE

Simplicity®

The mid-decade "mini-crini collection" from British designer Vivienne Westwood is likely a precursor to the Lacroix pouf. Westwood showed mini-length and bell-shaped "crinoline" skirts that were constructed much like the historic hoop skirts of the nineteenth century. Although these bouffant looks delivered a silhouette very similar to Lacroix's pouf, Westwood's mini-crinis did not enjoy the same commercial success.

Simplicity printed sewing
pattern #8347
1987
Compare with *City Lights Fashions* #664

#664
From the *City Lights Fashions* collection
1991
Worn by Beach Blast Barbie

175

The first Barbie pouf dress, Gay Parisienne, was released in 1959.

#964
Gay Parisienne
1959
Designed by Charlotte Johnson
Worn by Ponytail Barbie

176

Wild at *Heart*

The leather jacket has been a visual element of youthful rebellion for decades, with various subcultures employing it within their individual style identities. The symbolic legacy of this garment was hastened by popular musicians of the late 1980s and the 1990s. These curated style statements incorporated the leather-jacket theme and instigated a street-up trend that the fashion catwalks embraced.

Vogue magazine described the newest fashion trend: "Brando meets Madonna as black leather combines with fishnet, rap jewelry, pearls, and soft skirts for a sexy new look." Titled "Wild at Heart," the fashion article appeared in the issue dated September 1, 1991. Marlon Brando's iconic character in the 1953 film *The Wild One* informs both the *Vogue* article and the name given to the faux-leather-clad Barbie doll Wild Style. If Brando is credited with cementing the youthful-rebellion status of the biker jacket in popular American culture, then pop star Madonna should likely be credited for inciting the contemporary version of this trend during the late 1980s. The classic leather biker jacket had a starring role in her music video "Papa Don't Preach" and was used on stage in the "Who's That Girl World Tour." Madonna's unique styling of the classic signaled a rebellious innovator and furthered her tough-yet-feminine persona.

By the 1990s, the hip-hop music scene was a thriving lifestyle business. MTV's first episodic program dedicated to rap music and hip-hop culture debuted in the US in 1988. *Yo! MTV Raps* effectively positioned hip-hop in everyone's home and solidified the genre's mainstream success. Hip-hop music was central to the era's youth and was a predominant influence on clothing throughout the decade.

#0411
Original outfit for Wild Style Barbie
designed exclusively for Target
1992
Worn by Wild Style Barbie

During the late 1980s, a distinguishing garment worn by the women of Salt-N-Pepa was the oversized leather jacket. Perhaps the adoption of a garment famed for its counterculture tradition was a strategic selection by these ladies. Indeed, they were functioning as outsiders and rebels in a male-dominated hip-hop industry.

Wild Style Barbie offers two of Vogue's noted elements for the "Wild at Heart" trend. The ensemble offers a fine likeness of the classic black leather biker jacket with the "rap jewelry" component satisfied by the heavy, gold-tone, and chain-rope style necklace. This doll and her outfit affirm that the Mattel fashion designers are following the trends of popular culture.

This doll and her outfit affirm that the Mattel fashion designers are following the trends of popular culture.

Salt-N-Pepa
January 1987
Compare with the original outfit for
Wild Style Barbie

#0411
Original outfit for Wild Style Barbie
designed exclusively for Target
1992
Worn by Wild Style Barbie

As one the first all-female rap groups, Salt-N-Pepa is remembered as a trailblazing force within the male-dominated field. The group's fashionable look incorporated cherry-picked visual-heritage elements in service of a distinctive feminine image.

Twelve years following the introduction of rap music, Mattel acknowledges the mainstream popularity of the hip-hop genre. Rappin' Rockin' Barbie cautiously interprets the requisite style elements of the female rap artist: black leather jacket, cap with visor, hoodie blouse, sizable gold-tone pendant necklace, and hoop earrings.

Rappin' Rockin' Barbie cautiously interprets the requisite style elements of the 1980s female rap artist.

Salt-N-Pepa
November 1988
Compare with the original outfit for
Rappin' Rockin' Barbie

#3248
Original outfit for Rappin' Rockin'
Barbie
1992
Worn by Rappin' Rockin' Barbie

Who Are You Wearing?

Released in 1992, the new Barbie *Classique Collection* was developed specifically to launch the brand's collector division. These higher-price-point dolls were designed with the adult collector in mind and, as explained by Carol Spencer in her book *Dressing Barbie*, are "meant to display and not for play."

Clearly stated on the new product's packaging was a byline reading "by Carol Spencer." This was to be the first occurrence of an in-house Mattel designer garnering package-printed recognition for her design work. External fashion designers like Oscar de la Renta, Jean Paul Gaultier, and Thierry Mugler had received bylines crediting their work for Barbie, but an internal employee had not been duly acknowledged. The inclusion of the byline on the packaging was public affirmation of an individual employee's contribution to the brand and offered a behind-the-scenes component likely to be of interest to the collector-market connoisseurs.

During the 1990s, individual fashion designer names became more valuable to the consumer, with their brand's logos making prominent appearances on all manner of merchandise. These visually conspicuous brand statements served as a proof of purchase or a certificate of authenticity communicating the status and/or taste level of the end user. Perhaps this cultural sentiment informs Mattel's decision to mine the inherent value of its internal design talent.

A newfound interest in the players of the fashion industry, namely the fashion models and fashion designers, led to an informed audience of aficionados eager to follow along with all related intrigue. Capitalizing on the cultural curiosity, red-carpet preshow commentators posed a loaded question to the celebrity attendees, "Who are you wearing?"

#1618
Hollywood Premiere
1992
Design by Carol Spencer
Worn by Party Premiere Barbie

193

Life-size skirt suit
1989–1992
Design by Lillie Rubin
Compare with *Fifth Avenue Style*

Thierry Mugler's catwalk presentations during the late 1980s featured refined and sculpted jacket shapes emphasizing both feminine curves and dramatic angles. Corsets were often worn with these highly engineered looks to smooth, highlight, and contour the ideal silhouette. His modern jacket silhouettes launched a trend that was commercially successful well into the 1990s.

The Barbie outfit Fifth Avenue Style ensemble effectively mimics one of the designer's jacket silhouettes. The artistry required to translate the Mugler look into a Barbie-size scale is indeed impressive. Perhaps the canine companion is inspired by the dog models Mugler often sent down the catwalk during his fashion presentations.

The artistry required to translate the Mugler look into a Barbie-size scale is indeed impressive.

#1646
Fifth Avenue Style
1992
Design by Carol Spencer
Worn by Malaysian Barbie

Barbie fashion designers continue to keep pace with the couturiers of Europe during the 1990s. The doll's catwalk-inspired outfits highlight the unique technical skills that are required by the Mattel fashion team to translate these styles into looks that are recognizable when executed at the Barbie scale.

Couturier Yves Saint Laurent has served as an inspiration for the Mattel fashion design team since the 1960s. Continuing the tradition, Barbie released this distinctive *Haute Couture Fashions* ensemble influenced by the designer's catwalk offerings for the Autumn/Winter 1990–1991 collection. Predictably, the hue of Saint Laurent's jacket is substituted with a more Barbie-friendly bright violet.

Couturier Yves Saint Laurent has served as an inspiration for the Mattel fashion design team since the 1960s.

Design by Yves Saint Laurent
Autumn/Winter 1990–1991
Catwalk presentation: March 1990
Compare with *Haute Couture Fashions* #3847

#3847
From the *Haute Couture Fashions* collection
1992
Worn by Spanish Barbie

In 1988, Barbie scored her first Chanel skirt suit. Ten years later, she added the newest version of the classic to her closet. Chanel's iconic gold-chain belt and the suit's tweedy fabric are the featured design elements that serve as "Chanel-isms," signaling the refined status of the Barbie doll lifestyle.

Chanel suit
Design by Karl Lagerfeld for Chanel
Spring/Summer 1994
Catwalk presentation: October 1993
Compare with *Fashion Avenue-Internationale* #18108

#18108
From the *Fashion Avenue-Internationale* collection
1998
Worn by City Style Barbie

A rave is a large dance party with a curated ambience featuring performances by DJs and musicians playing electronic dance music. The attendees, known as ravers, embrace a distinctive ethos defined by their collective experience at these musical events. Originating in the late 1980s, rave culture enjoyed a global popularity by the youth of the era.

Raver fashion was, and is, a significant niche within the streetwear market. Loose-fitting garments affording all manner of dance moves are an important component of raver style. This baggy and forgiving pant featured extra-wide leg openings with huge rear pockets. Nicknamed "phat pants," the oversized and unisex silhouette offered pant legs potentially measuring an astonishing fifty inches in width.

Loose-fitting garments affording all manner of dance moves are an important component of raver style.

Phat pants were a memorable streetwear trend of the 1990s.
January 1995
Compare with the original outfit for Happenin' Hair Barbie

#22882
Original outfit for Happenin' Hair Barbie
1998
Worn by Happenin' Hair Barbie

Skaters and their characteristic clothing choices were an essential component of the Southern Californian surf scene. The streetwear market was built on the foundation established by this subculture. Rooted in the activewear clothing required when skateboarding, the skater look is defined by stylized versions of these traditional athletic garments.

Clothing from the heritage brand Adidas enjoys a cross-cultural appeal in the streetwear genre, as both the skaters and the hip-hop kids don the three-stripe detailing of the brand's iconic logo.

The streetwear market segment began as a niche movement but was quickly adopted by established fashion designers.

#26982
From the *Fashion Avenue Metro Styles* collection
2000
Worn by Glam 'n Groom Christie

Lady Miss Kier of Deee-Lite
January 1993
Compare with *Fashion Avenue-Metro Styles* #26982

The
Influencer

At the end of 2014, the Italian luxury brand Moschino, designed by Jeremy Scott, presented a collection inspired by one of his enduring muses, the Barbie doll. "I brought all of the Barbie elements to Moschino for the Spring/Summer 2015 collection," explains Scott.

The designer describes his creative direction for the collection to *Vogue* magazine: "Like every girl and gay boy, I loved Barbie. It's hard not to; she's practically perfect. She's a good big sister; she's had every job in the world [and] worn every outfit. And, it's just joyful! [She] and I share the same things: we just want to bring joy to people." Albeit nearly watered down to a cliché, but still no less flattering, the Moschino catwalk presentation featured plenty of joyful, playful, and pink-colored pieces worn by fashion models styled in exuberantly blonde Barbie-esque wigs.

The Barbie brand has shown a dedication to reflect the accepted stylistic themes of the zeitgeist. Since 1959, Barbie has lived through an immense number of fashionable trends and credit should be given to her designers, who were responsible for selecting and translating contemporary style statements in a manner that flatters the Barbie doll and her identity. The department's fashion direction was cultivated through observation of the work of professional couturiers and that of the creative youth operating at street level.

The 2014 Moschino collection represents a consequential and structural course shift. In an about-face, Jeremy Scott, for the Moschino brand, presented a fashion collection that was directly inspired by the Barbie doll and her wardrobe. Such is a deviation from the original Barbie-brand mantra dedicated to simply reflecting, rather than guiding, the spirit of the moment. This illustrates that, by this point in time, fifty-five years following the birth of Barbie, her identity has reached a cultural maturity wherein external imitation is both feasible and advantageous. Although Barbie doll's newly earned position as an influencer is atypical, it is not unexpected.

Jeremy Scott
February 2013

TONY DUQUETTE'S
DAWNRIDGE

HUTTON WILKINSON

PHOTOGRAPHS BY TIM STREET-PORTER

FOREWORD BY HAMISH BOWLES

ABRAMS, NEW YORK